Water Movers

Written

CONTENTS

Harcourt Achieve
Rigby · Saxon · Steck-Vaughn

www.HarcourtAchieve.com
1.800.531.5015

Water Movers

When you look in the sea and the ocean, or in ponds and rivers, you will find lots of different animals. All of these animals need to move through the water.

They can move by:
- pumping water from their bodies.
- using wind.
- using the currents of the seas and oceans.
- using suckers.
- using legs, feet, and a tail.

water strider

cuttlefish

water boatman

bluebottle

platypus

sea urchin

3

How Animals Move in Seas and Oceans

This animal is called a cuttlefish.
It can move in the water in different ways.

A cuttlefish can squirt a jet of water from its body.
It sucks water into its body and then squirts it out through
a tube called a siphon. The jet of water helps it move very
quickly. The cuttlefish also has a fin around its body. This
fin helps the cuttlefish swim and hover in the water.

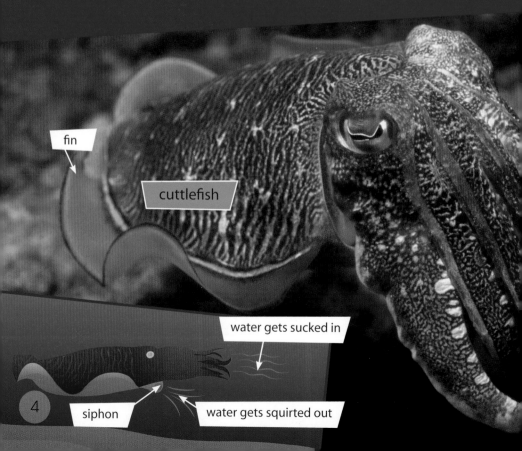

fin

cuttlefish

water gets sucked in

siphon

water gets squirted out

The nautilus moves just like the cuttlefish. It can pump a jet of water from its body, too. It also has a shell that can help it move in the water. Inside its shell are lots of little spaces. The spaces are called chambers. The nautilus can keep air inside these chambers. When the nautilus wants to go up in the water, it can put lots of air into the chambers. And when it wants to go down in the water, it can let out some of the air.

chambers for keeping air

nautilus

This animal is a bluebottle. It has a special sac on its body that is filled with gas. The top part of the sac is called the crest. It works like a sail on a yacht. The bluebottle uses the wind and the currents of the ocean to move it from one place to another.

crest

gas-filled sac

bluebottle

Info Box
Sometimes bluebottles can get washed up onto the beach by strong winds.

This animal is sometimes called the purple sailor. It also uses the wind and currents to move along in the water. It has a flat disc on the top of its body instead of having an air sac like the bluebottle. On top of the flat disc is a sail. Purple sailors can point their sails to the left or to the right.

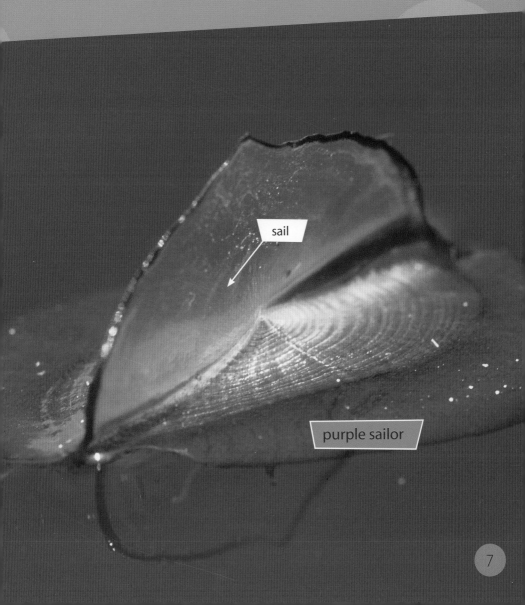

sail

purple sailor

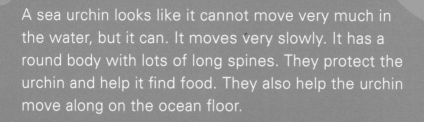

A sea urchin looks like it cannot move very much in the water, but it can. It moves very slowly. It has a round body with lots of long spines. They protect the urchin and help it find food. They also help the urchin move along on the ocean floor.

A sea urchin also has hundreds of tiny feet called tubes. The tubes have sticky suckers on them. The suckers help the sea urchin move along by holding on to whatever they touch.

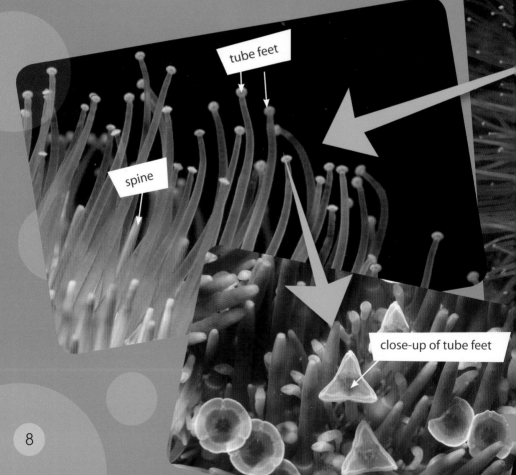

tube feet

spine

close-up of tube feet

sea urchin

How Animals Move in Ponds and Rivers

The backswimmer is an insect that gets its food under the water. Its back is shaped like the bottom of a boat and it has back legs that are very long. The backswimmer moves just below the surface of the water. It swims on its back and uses its back legs like the oars on a boat.

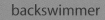
backswimmer

water boatman

This insect is called a water boatman. It also gets its food from under the water. It has two long back legs with lots of hairs on them. The legs are shaped like paddles, and they help the insect swim in the water.

A water strider can move very quickly on top of the water. It uses its front legs to grab food. It uses its middle legs to push its body forward, and its back legs to steer where it is going. It also has lots of tiny little hairs on its legs. The hairs trap air and help the water strider float on the water.

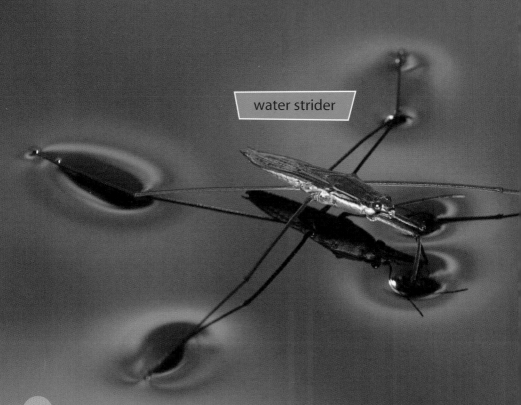

water strider

This animal is called a fish leech. It can swim and use its two suckers to help it move. The front sucker is also the leech's mouth. When a fish swims by, the fish leech grabs onto the fish with its mouth. The leech then moves in the water wherever the fish goes.

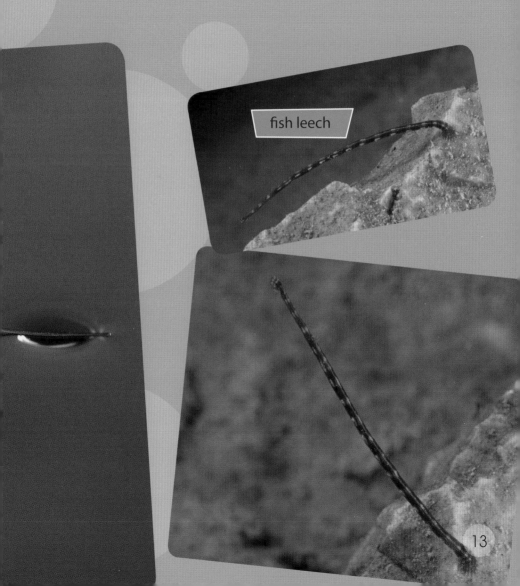

fish leech

The platypus can move on land and water. It is a very good underwater swimmer. It has webbed feet and a tail shaped like a paddle. It uses its front feet to pull it through the water, and its back feet and tail to steer and stop.

platypus

tail

webbed foot

Summary

Moving in Seas and Oceans

Cuttlefish
- pumps water from its body to move
- has a fin for swimming and hovering

Sea Urchin
- has spines to move on the ocean floor
- uses tube feet with suckers to move

Nautilus
- pumps water from its body to move
- uses air chambers to go up and down in the water

Bluebottle
- has a gas-filled sac with a crest like a sail
- uses the wind to move
- uses the currents to move

Moving in Ponds and Rivers

Backswimmer
- swims on its back
- uses its back legs like oars to move

Platypus
- uses its webbed feet to move
- uses its front feet to pull it through the water
- uses its back legs and tail to steer and stop

Water Boatman
- has two long back legs
- has hairs on its back legs that help it move
- uses its back legs like paddles to move

Water Strider
- uses its middle legs to push it forward on the water
- uses its back legs to steer where it is going
- has hairs on its legs that trap air to help it float on the water

Purple Sailor

- has a sail
- uses the wind
  to move
- uses the currents
  to move

Fish Leech

- can swim
- has two suckers,
  which it uses
  to move
- uses its front
  sucker to grab on
  to moving fish

Index

Explanations explain how things work and why things happen.

How to Write an Explanation:

Step One

- Choose a topic.
- Make a list of the things you know about the topic.

Topic:

Water Movers

What I know:

* The sea and river are full of animal that can move.

* Some animals move in the water with wind.

* Some animals move in the water using their bodies.

- Write down the things you need to find out.

What I would like to find out:

* How do animals move around in the water?

* How do animals use parts of their bodies to move in the water?

* What other animals move in the water and how do they do it?